What is a Sikh?

Twenty Questions about Sikhi and the Answers

BY SUKHWINDER KAUR BASRA

MW01529257

◆ FriesenPress

Suite 300 - 990 Fort St
Victoria, BC, V8V 3K2
Canada

www.friesenpress.com

Copyright © 2020 by Sukhwinder Kaur Basra
First Edition — 2020

with

Dr. Manjit Singh Hunjin (Amsimeet Art), Amrit Singh, Navjot Singh Sandhu (Singh Artworks), and Parm Singh (Calgary)

All rights reserved.

No part of this publication may be reproduced in any form, or by any means, electronic or mechanical, including photocopying, recording, or any information browsing, storage, or retrieval system, without permission in writing from FriesenPress.

ISBN
978-1-5255-6021-7 (Hardcover)
978-1-5255-6022-4 (Paperback)
978-1-5255-6023-1 (eBook)

1. RELIGION, SIKHISM

Distributed to the trade by The Ingram Book Company

1

What Is a Sikh?

The word *Sikh* means "to learn" in the Punjabi language.

Sikhs are students or followers of Guru Nanak Ji and the Sikh religion. The Sikh religion is called Sikhism or Sikhi.

The word *gu* means "darkness" and the word *ru* means "light," so *guru* means "giver of lightness/knowledge" or "spiritual teacher." *Ji* is used as a sign of respect when addressing an elder or person of authority.

Sikhs believe that there is only one god, known as *Vaheguru*, which means "wonderful teacher" or "light."

Some other names used by the Sikhs for god include, *Guru Sahib* (respected giver of light/knowledge), *Rabh* (lord), *Akal Purakh* (timeless being), *Sat Naam* (true name), *Paramatma* (main soul), and *Ik Onkar* (one creator).

To the Sikhs, Vaheguru is the creator of everything, is present in all living things, and guides and protects us.

Sikhi is the fifth-largest religion in the world. It is also one of the youngest world religions.

Sikhi is over 550 years old. There are about 26 million Sikhs around the world. Three million Sikhs live in 75 countries outside of India, and the rest live in India.

There are two main types of Sikhs. These are baptized Sikhs, known as *Amritdharis* (devoted followers), and non-baptized Sikhs, known as *Sahejdharis* (easy/ slow followers).

To become a baptized Sikh and be accepted into *Khalsa* (community of baptized Sikhs), you must take part in a Sikh baptism ceremony. This sacred ceremony, which is a very special event in a Sikh's life, is known as *Amrit Sanskar* (sweetened holy water ceremony).

Amrit Sanskar takes place at the Sikh temple and involves drinking *amrit* (sweetened holy water), which is presented by five previously baptized Sikhs, while *shabads* (verses) from the Sikh holy book are recited. The amrit is also sprinkled on the eyelids and the top of the head of the Sikh being baptized.

Amritdhari Sikhs must also commit to wearing the five articles of the Sikh faith, the 5Ks, and promise to follow the Sikh religious principles and rules according to the Sikh Code of Conduct.

There is no formal age for becoming a baptized Sikh. The ceremony can be performed at any time when a Sikh thinks he or she is ready.

2 Who Is Guru Nanak Ji?

Guru Nanak Ji is the founder of Sikhi. He is the first born of the ten gurus of Sikhi.

Guru Nanak Ji was born in 1469, in a village called Rai Bhoi di Talwandi, in Punjab. The village used to be part of India. It is now in present-day Pakistan.

Did you know that India, Pakistan, and Bangladesh were all one country before the former India was separated into different countries in 1947? This is also when Britain left India after ruling it for two hundred years.

Rai Bhoi di Talwandi is now known as Nankana Sahib, which translates to "the place where Nanak Ji came from."

The name of the province where Guru Nanak Ji was born is Punjab. The name means "land of five rivers." Guru Nanak Ji was born to a simple Hindu family. His father, Mehta Kalian Das, known as Mehta Kalu, was an accountant. His mother, Tripta Devi was a very religious woman.

Guru Nanak Ji also had an older sister named Nanaki. He was fond of her, and the siblings shared a special bond.

As a young boy, Guru Nanak Ji would give away his books, clothes, and food to the less fortunate.

Guru Nanak Ji was fascinated by the concept of god and religion. He would spend many hours meditating. He often discussed religion with both Hindu and Muslim teachers and followers.

By the age of sixteen, Guru Nanak Ji had learned many languages. He knew Sanskrit, Persian, Hindi, and Punjabi.

In 1487, Guru Nanak Ji married Sulakhni and they had two sons. They were named Sri Chand and Lakshmi Chand.

Guru Nanak Ji also had two very close friends. One of them was Bala, who was a Hindu. The other was Mardana, who was a Muslim. The religions of these two friends did not matter to Guru Nanak Ji. He believed that there is no Hindu and no Muslim, and that we are all children of Vaheguru. He believed that everyone is equal, even if they believe in different religions.

Guru Nanak Ji taught a message about love. He taught his followers to treat people equally regardless of their caste (social or occupational status), religion, appearance, race, and gender. He taught that there is only one Vaheguru who is present in all living things. Guru Nanak Ji spread the message of unity and service, and the principle of oneness of humanity (that all humans are equal because Vaheguru created everyone equally).

Guru Nanak Ji worked during the day as an accountant. In the early mornings and in the evenings, he would meditate and sing shabads while his friend Mardana played his *rabab* (a stringed instrument).

Each day, more and more people would gather around to listen to Guru Nanak Ji and Mardana performing shabads. These shabads became known as *Gurbani* (Guru's word). The crowds or followers became known as the Sikhs.

THE UDASIS (TRAVELS) OF GURU NANAK JI

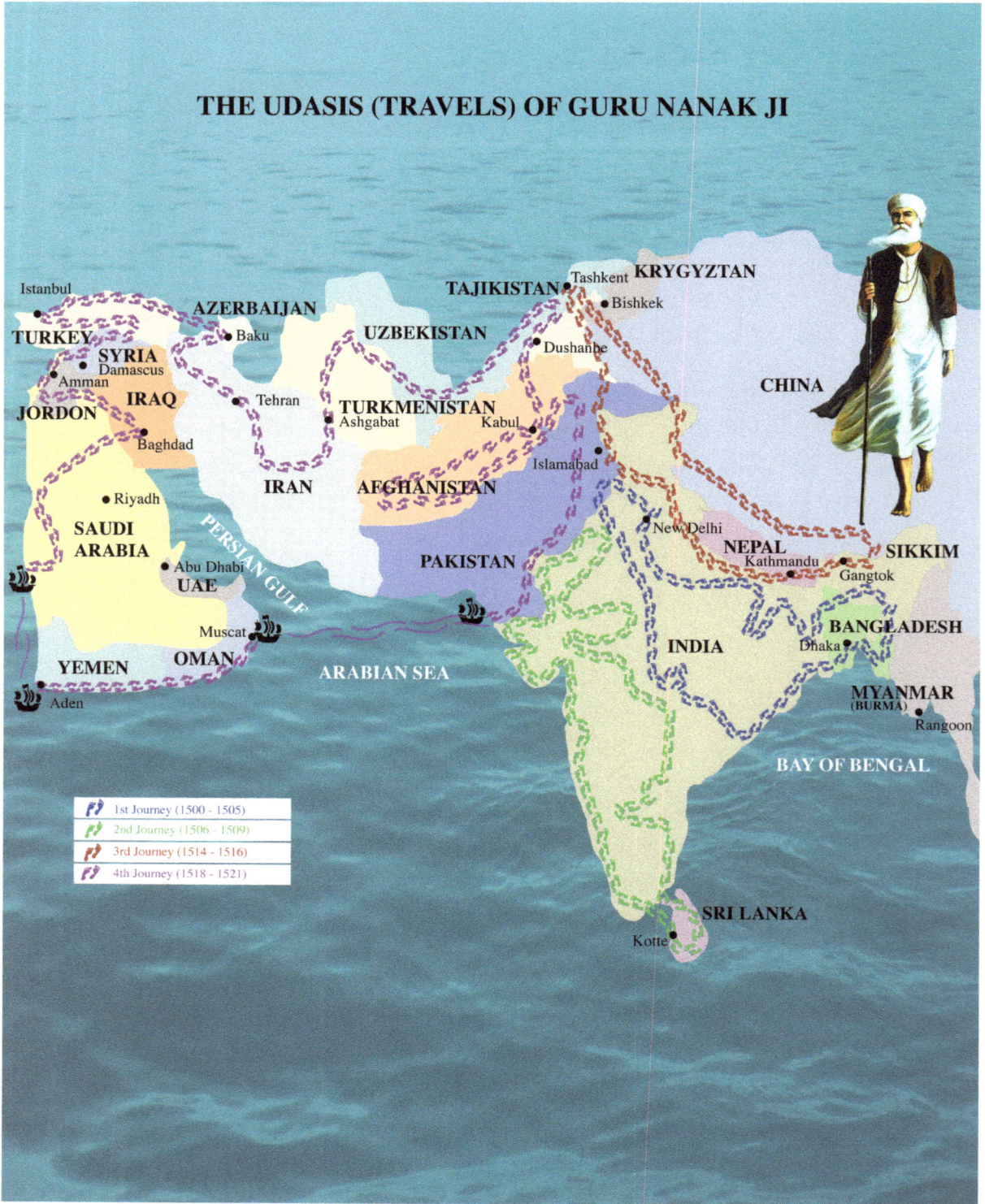

Legend:
- 1st Journey (1500 - 1505)
- 2nd Journey (1506 - 1509)
- 3rd Journey (1514 - 1516)
- 4th Journey (1518 - 1521)

Map labels:

Istanbul, TURKEY, AZERBAIJAN, Baku, SYRIA, Damascus, Amman, IRAQ, JORDON, Tehran, Baghdad, IRAN, Riyadh, SAUDI ARABIA, Abu Dhabi, UAE, Muscat, OMAN, YEMEN, Aden, PERSIAN GULF, ARABIAN SEA

UZBEKISTAN, Dushanbe, TURKMENISTAN, Ashgabat, Kabul, AFGHANISTAN, Islamabad, PAKISTAN, TAJIKISTAN, Tashkent, KRYGYZTAN, Bishkek, CHINA

New Delhi, NEPAL, Kathmandu, SIKKIM, Gangtok, BANGLADESH, Dhaka, INDIA, MYANMAR (BURMA), Rangoon, BAY OF BENGAL, SRI LANKA, Kotte

8

Guru Nanak Ji travelled far and wide on foot with his friend Mardana to convey his teachings.

It is believed that they made approximately four major journeys, spanning thousands of kilometers. They travelled all over India and as far as the Middle East.

After Guru Nanak Ji returned from his travels, he settled in Kartarpur (the city of Vaheguru) with his family. This is where the first Sikh community was created. This is also where Guru Nanak Ji built the first Sikh temple in 1521 and the community kitchen was introduced.

Kartarpur Sahib is located on the banks of the River Ravi at the border of Pakistan and India.

Before Guru Nanak Ji passed away in 1539 at the age of 70, he appointed his dedicated follower, Lehna, as the second Guru. As a symbol of his love for Lehna, Guru Nanak Ji renamed him Angad (my own limb).

In turn, the following nine Sikh Gurus would go on to appoint their successors.

What Does Sikhi Teach?

Sikhi has three main principles or values:

Kirat Karo	=	Work hard and earn an honest living.
Vand Ke Shako	=	Share with others. When possible, share 10% of your earnings with the needy, sick, and the less fortunate. This sharing of one's earnings/wealth is known as *Das Vand* (one-tenth shared).
Naam Japna	=	Name reciting. Always remember God (meditation).

Sikhs are reminded to stay away from the following *panj dosh* (five thieves), also known as *panj vicaar* (five weaknesses). These are known as the five thieves because they steal a person's good judgment:

Kaam	=	Urge. The need or impulse to do something that is wrong.
Krodh	=	Anger. Even though being angry is a natural emotion that everyone experiences, we should learn to manage and control our anger before we say or do something that we later regret.
Lobh	=	Greed or temptation. The desire to always want more of something (materialistic things) beyond what we need or use, or to want something that belongs to someone else.
Moh	=	Attachment. The desire to be constantly attached to materialistic things and people.
Ahankar	=	Pride or Ego. The feeling that we are more important than or superior to others.

To overcome these panj dosh or panj vicaar, Sikhs should learn to develop and practice the following *panj gunh* (five qualities) throughout their lifetime:

Sat	=	Truth. Not just speaking the truth, but also focusing on truthful living.
Pyar	=	Love. Keeping our minds full of love for Vaheguru and all of Vaheguru's creations. Focus on forgiveness and not having negative thoughts.
Santokh	=	Contentment. Being happy with what Vaheguru has blessed us and accepting Vaheguru's *hukam* (command or order).
Daya	=	Compassion. Being concerned and considerate about the suffering of others.
Nimrata	=	Humility. Being modest and avoiding thoughts that we are better or more important than others.

By developing and following these panj gunh, we become closer and more connected to Vaheguru. A Sikh's focus in life is to become *gurmukh* (god-centered) rather than *manmukh* (self-centered).

SYMBOLS OF SIKHI

IK ONKAR
(One Vaheguru or One Creator)

KHANDA
(The Swords of Wisdom)

THE CHAKKAR
(circle)
Represents that Vaheguru is
without a beginning or an end.
It also reminds the Sikhs to
follow the rules of Sikhi.

THE KHANDA
(double-edged sword)
Represents the belief in
Vaheguru and knowledge.

THE TWO KIRPANS
(two swords)
Represent the balance of everything
in life. They remind the Sikhs to protect
their faith, stand up for what is right, and
to live with equality and respect.

What Are the Symbols of Sikhi?

The symbols of Sikhi are as follows:

- **Ik Onkar** (one Vaheguru or one creator)

- **The Khanda** (the swords of wisdom)

Each part of the Khanda represents something special.

The *Khanda* (double-edged sword) represents the belief in one Vaheguru and knowledge.

The *Chakkar* (circle) represents that Vaheguru is without a beginning or an end. It also reminds the Sikhs to follow the rules of Sikhi.

The **two *Kirpans*** (swords) represent the balance of everything in life. "*Kirp*" means act of kindness/blessing and "*an*" means honor/respect. They remind the Sikhs to stand up for what is right, live with equality and respect, protect their faith, and be connected to Vaheguru.

The left sword is known as *Miri* (political) and the right sword is known as *Piri* (spiritual).

'SAT SHRI AKAL'

- **SAT**
means Truth

- **SHRI**
means Respected

- **AKAL**
means God

5 How Do Sikhs Greet Each Other?

The traditional greeting used by Sikhs is, *"Vaheguru ji ka Khalsa, Vaheguru ji ki fateh."* This greeting means "Sikhs belong to Wonderful God, victory belongs to Wonderful God."

Most Sikhs greet each other with *Sat Shri Akal* (Vaheguru is truth) instead.

When greeting another person, it is common practice for Sikhs to join their hands together in a prayer position. So, they lift their hands to the chest level, and put their palms together. This is to show respect to the other person while the name of Vaheguru is being said.

Where Do Sikhs Go to Worship?

Sikhs can worship at home or at the Sikh temple. A Sikh temple was originally known as a *dharamsala* (home of religious practice) but would later become known as a *gurdwara*. The word *gurdwara* means "doorway to Vaheguru."

The gurdwara is a place of worship. To the Sikhs, being a part of a sangat (congregation) is very significant. When we sit and pray together as equals, we become more connected and closer to Vaheguru.

Most gurdwaras are open twenty-four hours a day, seven days a week. Smoking, drugs, and alcohol are not allowed at the gurdwara.

All gurdwaras across the world always include the following:

Shri Guru Granth Sahib:	The Sikh holy book. It contains religious verses and scriptures.
Darbaar Sahib:	Hall of Vaheguru or prayer hall. This is a large room. The Shri Guru Granth Sahib is placed in this room when it is being read. There are no chairs and the floor is usually covered with carpet.
Langar:	Community kitchen. Food is served for free.
Chaar Dawar:	Four doors. The doors show that the gurdwara welcomes everyone from all castes, religions, appearances, races, and genders.
Nishaan Sahib:	A triangular yellow flag with the Khanda symbol. This flag is found outside the gurdwara, mounted on a high post. The Nishaan Sahib shows everyone near and far that the building is a gurdwara.

Every gurdwara also contains a separate room with a *manji* (bed). This room is known as *Sach Khand* (true home), and acts as a resting place for the Shri Guru Granth Sahib during the night.

19

The gurdwara is also a place to learn how to read and write the Punjabi language, learn how to play musical instruments such as the *baja* (harmonium) and *tabla* (drum), and to celebrate religious festivals, special occasions, and ceremonies.

The best-known gurdwara in the world is called Shri Harmandir Sahib (the holy abode/home of Vaheguru) and it is located in Amritsar, Punjab, India. It is also known as the Golden Temple because it is plated in gold. The Shri Harmandir Sahib is surrounded by *sarovar* (a pool of water).

The third guru, Guru Amar Das Ji, instructed the fourth guru, Guru Ram Das Ji, to start work on building the sarovar on land that had been donated by local businessmen.

The fifth guru, Guru Arjun Ji, completed the work on the sarovar and designed the Shri Harmandir Sahib. He placed it on a lower level, so that even the proudest person had to step down before entering the gurdwara. This is to remind everyone to be humble before Vaheguru.

As a sign of respect for all religions, the foundation stone for the gurdwara was laid by a famous Muslim religious leader called Mian Mir. This gurdwara was completed in 1604.

In 1764, the Shri Harmandir Sahib was rebuilt by a well-known Sikh leader named Jassa Singh Ahluwalia. He had the help of other Sikh leaders and volunteers, and he collected a lot of donations.

During his rule from 1802 to 1831, the first king of Punjab, Maharaja Ranjit Singh, had the Shri Harmandir Sahib decorated with marble sculptures, gold, and large quantities of precious stones.

The Shri Harmandir Sahib is one of the holiest and most sacred places for Sikhs. It is also considered the seventh wonder of India.

Did you know that there are about 30,000 gurdwaras in India, and thousands of gurdwaras all around the world? You may even have a gurdwara very close to you.

What Is the Shri Guru Granth Sahib?

The words *Shri Guru Granth Sahib* mean respected holy teacher book. It is a book that contains shabads and scriptures written and composed by the Sikh gurus. The Shri Guru Granth Sahib is considered to be the living guru for the Sikhs.

It was originally known as the *Adi Granth Sahib* (first respected book). It was renamed Shri Guru Granth Sahib by the tenth guru, Guru Gobind Singh Ji.

The Shri Guru Granth Sahib contains 1,430 *angs* (pages) and 6,000 shabads. It is written in *Gurmukhi*. The word *Gurmukhi* means "from the Guru's mouth." The shabads are poetic and are read in a rhythmic form, known as *raag* (beauty or colour).

Gurmukhi is a type of script used to write the Punjabi language. It was created by the second guru, Guru Angad Ji.

It takes about forty-eight hours to read the entire Shri Guru Granth Sahib without interruption. The recitation is done so that others can listen to it. People usually take turns during the recitation. When one person gets tired, another takes over. This way the recitation remains uninterrupted. This reciting of prayers is known as an *Akhand Paath* (uninterrupted reading).

When the Shri Guru Granth Sahib is read over a period of forty-eight hours, then it is known as a *Sahej Paath* (easy/slow reading). A Sahej Paath can be completed over ten days.

A *paath* (reading) takes place during religious festivals, special occasions, and ceremonies. It is considered a very holy practice and is said to bring peace to the entire sangat.

CHANANI
(shade or cover)

PALKI
(canopy)

CHAUR SAHIB
(fan)

TAKHT
(raised platform or seat
of authority)

SHRI GURU
GRANTH SAHIB
(Sikh holy book)

MANJI
(bed)

RUMALA
(decorative cloth)

GOLAK
(cash/donation box)

8 Where Is the Shri Guru Granth Sahib Stored?

During the day, the Shri Guru Granth Sahib is placed at the Darbaar Sahib on top of the manji, which sits on a raised platform, known as a *takht* (throne or seat of authority). It is placed on a higher level as a sign of respect.

The takht is then placed under the *palki* (canopy). This structure represents the importance of the Shri Guru Granth Sahib.

The *chanani* (shade or cover) is draped above the palki and takht and is attached to the ceiling. This shade or cover is a sign of the utmost respect for the Shri Guru Granth Sahib.

The Shri Guru Granth Sahib itself is kept covered with a *rumala* (a decorative cloth) when it is not being read.

Each morning, Sikhs take the Shri Guru Granth Sahib from the Sach Khand and carry it to the takht. Each night, Sikhs take the Shri Guru Granth Sahib from the takht and carry it back to the Sach Khand.

This is symbolic. It shows that the Sikhs treat and respect the Shri Guru Granth Sahib as a living guru.

The original Shri Guru Granth Sahib is kept at the Shri Harmandir Sahib.

Some baptized Sikhs keep a copy of the Shri Guru Granth Sahib in a separate room in their homes. Others keep smaller versions called *gutkas* (to guard or protect). Gutkas contain a selection of daily shabads from the Shri Guru Granth Sahib.

9 What Do We Do When We Arrive at the Gurdwara?

When we visit the gurdwara, we should wear conservative and loose clothes, so we can sit comfortably on the floor.

When we arrive at the gurdwara, we should do the following:

- Cover our heads

- Take our shoes off

- Wash our hands

- Give offerings

- Bow down in front of the Shri Guru Granth Sahib

Why Do We Cover Our Heads When Entering the Gurdwara?

Did you know that people from other religions also cover their heads while praying?

Sikhs believe that most of the body's energy is held at the top of the head. This top center of the head is a focal point of energy. It is known as the crown chakra.

Whenever we are in the presence of the Shri Guru Granth Sahib, Vaheguru gives us energy. That energy is sacred. When we retain it, Vaheguru's energy lives inside of us. We cover our heads to manage and honor this sacred energy.

Remember that the Shri Guru Granth Sahib is considered to be the living guru for the Sikhs. Keeping our heads covered also shows humility and submission to someone who is more powerful than us and worthy of respect.

Another key benefit of keeping our heads covered is that it protects our head from the elements. The head covering keeps our hair protected and clean.

Visitors without a turban or *dupatta* (ladies' scarf) to cover their heads can borrow a large handkerchief. These handkerchiefs are usually available at the gurdwara's entrance. This large handkerchief can be placed on top of the head and tied at the back with a large knot.

11 Why Do We Take Our Shoes Off?

We take our shoes off at the gurdwara and place them at the racks provided.

This is done to keep the area of the Darbaar Sahib clean. Also, because we have to sit on the floor, it is more comfortable to sit without our shoes on. When we sit comfortably, we can focus more clearly on Vaheguru's teachings. When we sit on the floor, we are sitting with the rest of the sangat on one level. This represents equality and unity.

Removing our shoes before we enter the Darbaar Sahib is respectful. Our shoes collect dirt from outside. We show respect by not bringing the dirt to a place where the sangat is sitting and serving. The place is a sacred space, and we must keep it clean. This also reminds us that we need to have a clean mind and heart when we are receiving Vaheguru's teachings.

Why Do We Give Offerings or Gifts?

When we arrive in front of the Shri Guru Granth Sahib, we place an offering of food or money on the mat or into the *golak* (cash box). This offering or gift is used to maintain the gurdwara and the community kitchen.

Seva (selfless/community service) is considered to be a very important concept for Sikhs.

This offering or gift is not considered charity. It is a sharing of Vaheguru's gifts with which we have been blessed.

Why Do We Bow Down to the Shri Guru Granth Sahib?

Once we have placed our offering or gift on the mat in front of the Shri Guru Granth Sahib, we get on our knees, bow down, and touch our forehead to the floor. This is known as *mutha tekh* (forehead touch) and is a sign of love and respect for Vaheguru.

By bowing down in front of the Shri Guru Granth Sahib, we admit that we know nothing and are asking Vaheguru for knowledge and blessing.

We can then sit quietly in the Darbaar Sahib with the rest of the sangat. Sitting together shows equality and humility. It is customary for women to sit on the left and men to sit on the right.

We should be careful not to point our feet toward the Shri Guru Granth Sahib or sit with our backs to it.

14 What Else Takes Place at the Gurdwara?

The gurdwara is a place where religious festivals, special occasions, and ceremonies take place.

These important events are performed in the presence of the Shri Guru Granth Sahib and a paath is read by the *granthi* (reader). These important events include the following:

- Birth or naming ceremony, known as *Naam Karan* (name create). When a child is born into a Sikh family, the family visits the gurdwara. The first letter of the child's name is selected with help from the Shri Guru Granth Sahib.
  Do you know what your name means? Do you know how your parents chose your name?

- Baptism ceremony, known as *Amrit Sanskar* (sweetened holy water ceremony).

- Marriage ceremony, known as *Anand Karaj* (blissful union).

- Funeral ceremony, known as *Antam Sanskar* (final rite).

- The Sikh gurus' birthdays, known as *Gurpurabs* and other important events in Sikh history, such as the creation of Khalsa.

After the completion of the paath, all the sangat in the Darbaar Sahib stands up, and the granthi completes a formal prayer known as *Ardas* (humble request or ask).

Ardas is a prayer that involves remembering Vaheguru and the ten Sikh gurus. This is also where we ask Vaheguru to bless the Sikhs and all humanity.

Upon completion of Ardas, all the sangat mutha tekh again and return to their sitting position.

Once the sangat is seated, a *Hukamnama* (Vaheguru's order/message) is read out aloud. The Hukamnama is a verse selected randomly by the granthi. The granthi will open a random place in the Shri Guru Granth Sahib and recite the first verse on the left-hand page. This is considered to be Vaheguru's message for the sangat.

After Hukamnama, the granthi and *sevadar* (volunteer) will go around the Darbaar Sahib to serve the *karah parsaad* (dessert/gracious gift) to all the sangat, while everyone remains seated. Karah parsaad is served to the sangat as a sign of equality and unity. It also shows that no one leaves Vaheguru's presence empty-handed.

The person being offered karah parsaad should accept it in a seated position. They should cup their hands and raise them high to help the sevadar serve them with ease. The karah parsaad can be transferred to the palm of one hand and eaten with the other hand.

Other events that also take place at the gurdwara include the following:

- **Kirtan** is when the sangat sings and recites shabads from the Shri Guru Granth Sahib.

- **Katha** is when the granthi recites and explains the writings and teachings of the Shri Guru Granth Sahib to the sangat.

- **Langar** is the shared free meal offered to everyone who attends the gurdwara.

15

Who Reads the Shri Guru Granth Sahib?

A granthi reads the Shri Guru Granth Sahib. A granthi can be a man or a woman, but needs to be a Sikh. He or she must be able to read Gurmukhi. It is believed that the first granthi in history was Baba Buddha Ji.

During the service, the granthi will sit on the takht and read from the Shri Guru Granth Sahib, and he or she will wave a *chaur sahib* (a type of fan) over the Shri Guru Granth Sahib.

A chaur sahib is usually made of fake hair and has a wooden or silver handle.

The chaur sahib is waved above the Shri Guru Granth Sahib to purify the area while the Shri Guru Granth Sahib is being read. This is done as a sign of respect for the Shri Guru Granth Sahib.

2. GURU ANGAD JI

1. GURU NANAK JI

3. GURU AMAR DAS JI

4. GURU RAM DAS JI

5. GURU ARJUN DEV JI

6. GURU HARGOBIND JI

7. GURU HAR RAI JI

8. GURU HARKRISHAN JI

9. GURU TEG BAHADUR JI

10. GURU GOBIND SINGH JI

16 Who Wrote the Shri Guru Granth Sahib?

Even though all the ten Sikh gurus made important contributions to Sikhi, the Shri Guru Granth Sahib was composed by only seven of the ten Sikh gurus. In the following list, the names in **red** are the names of the Sikh gurus who composed the Shri Guru Granth Sahib.

Guru Nanak Ji
Guru Angad Ji
Guru Amar Das Ji
Guru Ram Das Ji
Guru Arjun Dev Ji
Guru Hargobind Ji
Guru Har Rai Ji
Guru Harkrishan Ji
Guru Teg Bahadur Ji
Guru Gobind Singh Ji

The Shri Guru Granth Sahib also includes the writings of teachers of both Hinduism and Islam.

In 1604, the fifth guru, Guru Arjun Ji, put the Adi Granth Sahib together. This was done at the city of Amritsar, Punjab, India.

In 1708, the tenth Guru, Guru Gobind Singh Ji, said that he would be the last human guru and that the Shri Guru Granth Sahib would become the eternal living guru of the Sikhs. Guru Gobind Singh Ji instructed the Sikhs to turn to the Shri Guru Granth Sahib for guidance, support, and questions about Vaheguru.

What Are the 5Ks?

In 1699, during the celebration of *Vaisakhi* (harvest festival) at the village of Anandpur Sahib (place of happiness), Punjab, India, the tenth guru, Guru Gobind Rai (as he was known at that time), invited a large group of people to hear the words of Vaheguru.

Guru Gobind Rai requested volunteers from the sangat who would be willing to give up their lives at any time to protect the name of Vaheguru and defend the weak and less fortunate. The following five brave men, all from different castes, backgrounds, and faiths, came forward and volunteered to sacrifice their lives in the name of Vaheguru:

Daya Ram, a shopkeeper
Dharam Das, a farmer
Himmat Rai, a water-bearer
Mohkam Chand, a tailor
Sahib Chand, a barber

Guru Gobind Rai filled an iron bowl with water. He started to stir it with a double-edged sword known as a Khanda, while shabads were recited. This represented the need for strength. Meanwhile, his wife, Mata Sahib Ji, added a handful of sugar crystals into the iron bowl. The sugar represented that a person's strength should always be balanced by sweetness and kindness.

This sweetened water became known as amrit or *Khanda da Pahul* (rights of the sword).

PANJ KAKKAAR (5Ks)
(ARTICLES OF SIKH FAITH)

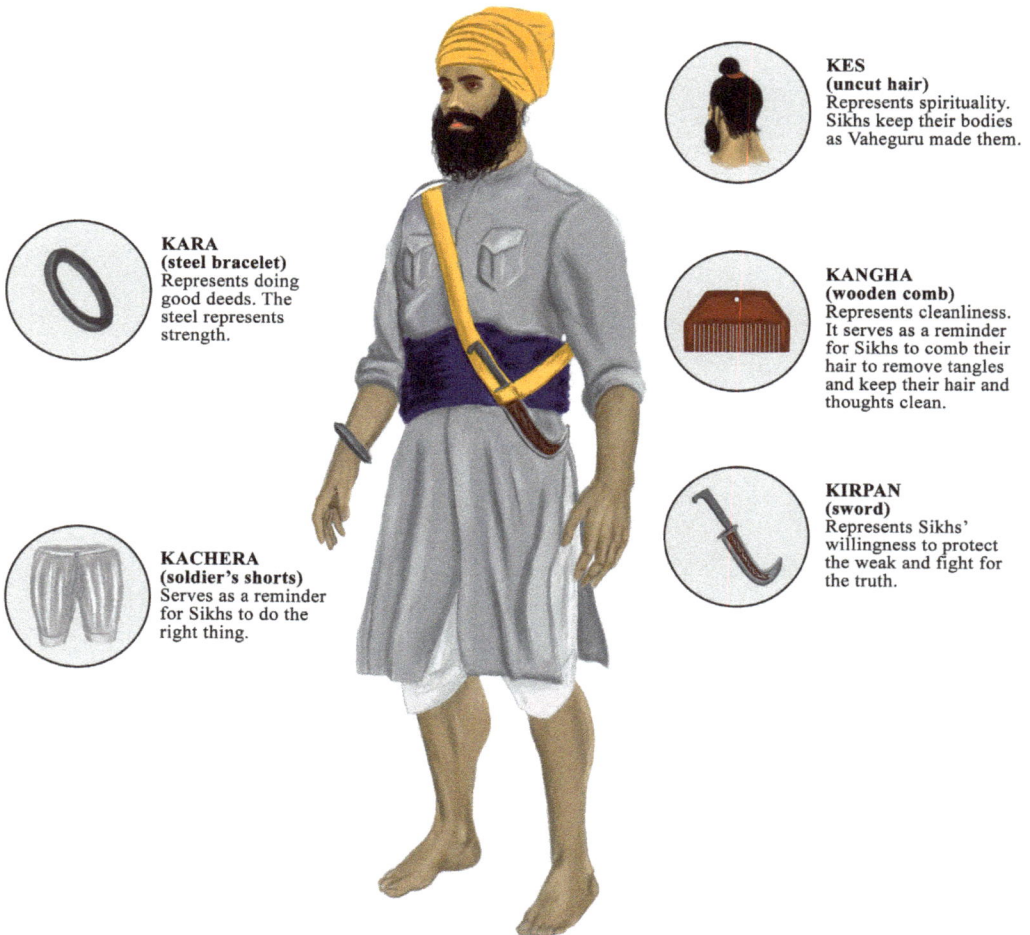

KES
(uncut hair)
Represents spirituality. Sikhs keep their bodies as Vaheguru made them.

KARA
(steel bracelet)
Represents doing good deeds. The steel represents strength.

KANGHA
(wooden comb)
Represents cleanliness. It serves as a reminder for Sikhs to comb their hair to remove tangles and keep their hair and thoughts clean.

KACHERA
(soldier's shorts)
Serves as a reminder for Sikhs to do the right thing.

KIRPAN
(sword)
Represents Sikhs' willingness to protect the weak and fight for the truth.

The five brave men drank the amrit from the iron bowl. They were lovingly called *Panj Pyare* (five beloved ones) by Guru Gobind Rai. They were further instructed to embrace a unique identity that would involve wearing a special type of uniform. This uniform became known as the five articles of the Sikh faith. These were called the *Panj Kakkar* or the 5Ks. The items would identify them as Sikh Warriors.

The Panj Kakkar are referred to as the 5Ks because the names of all the items begin with the Gurmukhi letter for K.

The Panj Kakkar or 5Ks are the following:

Kes: This is a person's uncut hair. Kes represents spirituality. Sikhs keep their bodies the way Vaheguru made them.

Sikh men and women wear a head covering known as a *dastaar* (hand of god) or *pagh* (turban) to cover their long, uncut hair and to protect it from dirt and dust. Sikh children wear a head covering known as a *patka*.

No one knows the true origins of the turban. It can be seen throughout countries in South and Central Asia, and in North and West Africa. Each culture has its specific style and reasons for wearing one.

Sikhs regard the dastaar as an important part of the Sikh identity and culture.

Kangha: This is a small wooden comb that represents cleanliness.

The small comb is worn in the hair and serves as a reminder for Sikhs to keep their thoughts clean, just as they comb their hair to remove the tangles and keep their hair clean.

Kara: This is a steel bracelet that represents doing good deeds.

The kara is made of steel to represent strength.

The kara is a circular shape to remind Sikhs that Vaheguru is without a beginning or an end.

The kara is worn around the wrist of the dominant arm (left or right hand) of the person and serves as a reminder to do good deeds.

The last two Ks are a reminder that Sikhs will protect the weak and fight for honesty.

Kirpan: This is a curved dagger that represents a sword. It shows Sikhs' willingness to protect the weak and to fight for the truth.

Kachera: This is an undergarment, also referred to as soldiers' shorts. It serves as a reminder for Sikhs to do the right thing.

Guru Gobind Rai requested that these men follow the Sikhi teachings and believe in one Vaheguru. They were to love Him, place their trust in Him, and remember Him always. They were also to consider everyone as equal, regardless of their caste, religion, appearance, race, and gender.

In turn, Guru Gobind Rai proceeded to drink the amrit himself. He wanted to show that even though he was a guru, everyone is equal in the eyes of Vaheguru. Eventually, one by one, other people from the sangat also took amrit that day and were baptized.

As another sign of equality, Guru Gobind Rai informed all the now-baptized Sikhs that their last names would be changed. Having the same last name would remove any reference to their caste or faith.

The common last name shows that they belong to one big family or community. This one big family or community would now be identified as Khalsa (the pure or belonging to).

Women were given the name *Kaur* (princess) to show dignity. Men were given the name *Singh* (lion) as a reminder of the need for courage and bravery.

Guru Gobind Rai also changed his name to Guru Gobind Singh that day.

This was a significant event in Sikh history and is referred to as the birth or creation of Khalsa.

This event is still celebrated today by Sikhs around the world during the festival of Vaisakhi. The festival takes place around April 13 every year. You may have taken part in Vaisakhi celebrations, too.

Can You Still Be a Sikh If You Have Not Taken Amrit?

A Sikh is defined as one who has been baptized and wears the 5Ks. This description is included in the *Rehat Maryada* (the Sikh Code of Conduct). This is the code developed in 1945 by the elected governing body for the world's gurdwaras, the Shiromani Gurdwara Parbandhak Committee. This organization makes all of the rules for Sikhi.

A Sahejdhari, a Sikh who has not taken amrit and does not wear the 5Ks, is still permitted to practice the Sikh religion and follow the Sikh principles.

This simply means that the person has chosen the path of Sikhi and follows the principles of the Sikh faith and the teachings of the Sikh gurus, but has not been baptized yet.

A Sahejdhari Sikh's aim should be to take amrit one day as it was Guru Gobind Singh Ji's request.

Like most religions, Sikhi is divided into strict and non-strict streams. How you choose to practice it depends on you.

You will see that most Sahejdhari Sikhs often wear one or more of the 5Ks, such as a kara or a dastaar.

What Is Langar?

Langar is the word used by the Sikhs for the community kitchen and the free meal served at the gurdwara.

All meals served at the gurdwara are vegetarian. The meal is designed so that everyone can eat together regardless of their faith and no one will be offended.

The langar is prepared, cooked, and served by volunteers. These volunteers also make sure that the langar is kept clean.

Langar is a symbol of the equality of humanity. People from all castes, religions, appearances, races, and genders are welcome. This is where everyone can sit and eat together as equals. This sitting and eating together without discrimination is known as *pangat* (row/line or group).

How Can I Pray?

As one of the main principles of Sikhi is *Naam Japna* (always remembering Vaheguru), we should engage in a daily practice of meditation by reciting Vaheguru's name.

By reciting the word Vaheguru, we are thanking Vaheguru for all the wonderful gifts we have been blessed with. This includes the universe, the world that we live in, the air that we breathe, our bodies and health, our family and friends, food and shelter, and all of Vaheguru's amazing creations.

When we meditate by reciting and repeating Vaheguru's name, it helps us to concentrate and not be distracted. We can meditate at any time of the day. However, the most effective time is the morning. Morning meditation is known as *Amrit Vela* (sweet nectar time).

To do this, observe the following:

- Set aside five or more minutes each day to meditate
- Find a quiet spot in your home, and cover your head with a scarf or dupatta
- Sit cross-legged on the floor, shoulders relaxed, and spine straight
- Place your hands in a prayer position (lift your hands to the chest level and put your palms together) or rest them on your lap
- If you prefer, you can close your eyes
- Relax your body and begin to take deep breaths in and out through your nose
- Be thankful for all Vaheguru's blessings
- Take a deep breath through your nose, feel your chest rise
- Slowly breathe out through your nose, feel your chest drop
- Take a deep breath through your nose, feel your chest rise
- Slowly breathe out through your nose and recite the word Vaheguru
- Continue to take deep breaths in and out through your nose
- With each breath out recite and repeat the word Vaheguru

We can also learn and recite the first Gurbani in the Shri Guru Granth Sahib. This Gurbani is called the *Mool Mantar* (root or beginning teaching).

The Mool Mantar

Ik Onkar
(ek on-kar)
There is one Vaheguru

Sat Naam
(sat n-aam)
Whose name is truth

Karta Purakh
(kar-ta poo-rakh)
Who is the Creator, present in all creations

Nirbhao, Nirvair
(ner-bho, ner-vair)
Who is without fear, without hate

Akal Moorat
(a-kaal moo-rat)
Who is timeless, without form

Ajooni Saibhang
(a-jooni sai-bhang)
Who is beyond birth and death, the enlightened one

Gur Parsaad
(gu-r par-saad)
Who can be known by the Guru's grace

Jap
(j-ap)
Chant and meditate

Aad Sach
(aa-d s-ach)
Who was true in the beginning

Jugaad Sach
(ju-gaad s-ach)
Who has been true throughout the ages

Hai Bhee Sach
(h-ai be s-ach)
Who is true now

Nanak Hosi Bhee Sach
(na-nak ho-see be s-ach)
Nanak says, who will always be true

Glossary/Pronunciation

Adi Granth Sahib
(a-dee gr-aanth saa-hib)

First respected book. Refers to the first scripture of the Sikh holy book.

Ahankar
(aa-hun-kaar)

Pride or ego. Refers to one of the five thieves/weaknesses that Sikhs should stay away from.

Akal Purakh
(a-kaal pu-rakh)

Timeless being. Refers to the name used by the Sikhs for God.

Akhand Paath
(a-khund p-aath)

Uninterrupted reading of the Sikh holy book.

Amrit
(um-rit)

Sweet holy water prepared while reciting the verses of the Sikh holy book and stirring with double-edged sword.

Amrit Sanskar
(um-rit san-skaa-r)

Sikh baptism. Refers to the sacred ceremony that Sikhs undertake to become part of the community of Khalsa (pure ones).

Amrit Vela
(um-rit vel-a)

Sweet nectar time. Refers to early morning meditation.

Amritdhari
(um-rit-daari)

Devoted follower of the Sikh religion. Refers to a baptized Sikh.

Anand Karaj
(a-nand ka-raj)

Blissful union. Refers to the Sikh marriage ceremony.

Angs (ung-s)	Limbs. Refers to the pages in the Shri Guru Granth Sahib.
Antam Sanskar (an-tam san-skaa-r)	Final rite. Refers to the Sikh funeral ceremony.
Ardas (ar-daas)	Humble request or ask. Refers to the formal prayer that takes place at the beginning or conclusion of a special ceremony/event.
Baja (ba-ja)	Harmonium.
Chaar Dawar (ch-aar da-var)	Four doors. Refers to all Sikh temples being open to everyone from all religions, backgrounds, occupations, and genders.
Chakkar (chak-kar)	Circle. Refers to the circle in the middle of the Sikh symbol known as a Khanda.
Chanani (cha-nani)	Shade or cover. Refers to the embellished canopy, which is usually attached to the ceiling and drapes over the area where the Sikh holy book is placed at the main prayer hall.
Chaur sahib (ch-aur sa-hib)	A type of fan.
Darbaar Sahib (dur-baar saa-hib)	Hall of the Guru/God or prayer hall.
Das Vand (d-as v-and)	One-tenth shared. Refers to sharing 10% of our earning/ wealth with the needy, sick, and less fortunate.
Dastaar (dus-taar)	The hand of god. Refers to the head covering worn by Sikhs. Also known as a pagh (turban).

Daya (dai-a)	Compassion. Refers to one of the five qualities that Sikhs must try to develop in their lifetime.
Dharamsala (dha-ram-sal-a)	Home of religious practice. Refers to the ancient name used to describe a Sikh temple.
Dupatta (du-pat-ta)	Ladies' scarf.
Golak (go-luck)	Cash box.
Granthi (graan-thi)	Reader. Refers to the person who reads the Sikh holy book.
Gurbani (gur-baani)	Guru's word. Refers to the religious verses composed by the Sikh Gurus and other writers of the Sikh holy book.
Gurdwara (gurd-waara)	Doorway to God. It is the name of the Sikh Temple.
Gurmukh (gur-mu-kh)	Facing God. Refers to the Sikhs being God-centered rather than self-centered.
Gurmukhi (gur-mu-khee)	From the mouth of the Guru. Refers to the type of script used to write the Punjabi language.
Gurpurab (gur-pu-rab)	Sikh Guru's birthday.
Guru (goo-roo)	*Gu* means darkness and the word *ru* means light. Refers to the giver of lightness/knowledge or spiritual teacher.
Guru Sahib (goo-roo saa-hib)	Respected giver of light/knowledge or spiritual teacher. Refers to the name used by the Sikhs for God.
Gutka (goot-ka)	To guard or protect. Refers to the smaller version of the Sikh holy book.

Hukam (hoo-kum)	Vaheguru's order or command.
Hukamnama (hoo-kum-nama)	Vaheguru's order or command/message. Refers to the reading of a randomly selected page from the Sikh holy book at the conclusion of a ceremony.
Ik Onkar (ek on-kar)	One God or one creator.
Ji (jee)	Punjabi term used as a sign of respect, added to the end of a name.
Kaam k-aam)	Urge. Refers to one of the five thieves/weaknesses that Sikhs should stay away from.
Kachera (kach-era)	Undergarment. Also known as soldiers' shorts. Refers to one of the five articles of faith that a baptized Sikh must wear. It serves a reminder for Sikhs to do the right thing.
Kangha (kun-ga)	Comb. Refers to one of the five articles of faith that a baptized Sikh must wear. The comb represents cleanliness and acts as a reminder for Sikhs to keep their minds clean.
Kara (ka-ra)	Steel bracelet. Refers to one of the five articles of faith that a baptized Sikh must wear. It represents doing good deeds. Steel represents strength. The circular shape serves as a reminder that God is without a beginning or end.

Karah parsaad (kar-raah pur-shaad)	Pudding-like dessert made from equal parts of flour, butter, sugar, and water. It is served at the conclusion of a religious ceremony in the presence of the Sikh holy book. It represents equality of all visitors at the Sikh temple.
Kartarpur Sahib (kar-tar-pur)	The city of God.
Katha (ka-tha)	Recitation and explanation of the writings and teachings of the Sikh holy book.
Kaur (Kor)	Princess. Refers to the middle or surname of all Sikh women.
Kes (k-ais)	Uncut hair. Refers to one of the five articles of faith that a baptized Sikh must wear. It represents spirituality and that Sikhs should keep their bodies the way God made them.
Khalsa (khal-sa)	The pure one. Refers to the group or community of baptized Sikhs.
Khanda (khun-da)	Double-edged sword. Refers to one of the Sikh symbols.
Khanda da Pahul (khund-a da pa-hul)	Sweet holy water prepared while reciting the verses of the Sikh holy book and stirring with a double-edged sword. It is also called amrit.
Kirat Karo (kee-rut ka-ro)	Work hard and earn an honest leaving. Refers to one of the three main Sikh principles or values.

Kirpan (keer-pan)	*Kirp* means act of kindness/blessing and *an* means honc respect. A curved dagger that represents a sword. Refers to one of the five articles of faith that a baptized Sikh must wear. It represents Sikhs' willingness to protect the weak and fight for the truth.
Kirtan (keer-tan)	Singing and reciting of the verses from the Sikh holy book by the congregation.
Krodh (kr-oadh)	Anger. Refers to one of the five thieves/weaknesses that Sikhs should stay away from.
Langar (lung-ar)	Community kitchen. It also refers to the free meal serve at the community kitchen found at all Sikh temples.
Lobh (loab)	Greed. Refers to one of the five thieves/weaknesses that Sikhs should stay away from.
Maharaja (ma-ha-ra-ja)	King.
Manji (maan-jee)	A stool or string bed.
Manmukh (man-mu-kh)	Facing me. Refers to the Sikhs moving from being self- centered to being God-centered.
Miri (mee-ree)	Political. Refers to the left sword found on the Sikh symbol known as the Khanda.
Moh (m-oh)	Attachment. Refers to one of the five thieves/weaknesse that Sikhs should stay away from.
Mool Mantar (m-ool man-tar)	Root or beginning teaching. Refers to the first verse in the Sikh holy book.
Mutha tekh (mu-tha taik)	Forehead touch. Refers to the bowing down and touching head to ground in front of the Sikh holy book.

Naam Japna (N-aam Jup-na)	Name reciting. Refers to always remembering God (meditation). Refers to one of the three main Sikh principles or values.
Naam Karan (n-aam ka-run)	Name create. Refers to the Sikh naming ceremony.
Nankana Sahib (naan-ka-na sa-hib)	The place where Guru Nanak Ji came from.
Nimrata (nim-rata)	Humility. Refers to one of the five qualities that Sikhs must try to develop in their lifetime
Nishaan Sahib (nee-shaan saa-hib)	The official flag of the Sikhs.
Paath (p-aath)	Reading. Refers to the reading from the Sikh holy book.
Pagh (p-ug)	Turban. Also known as a dastaar.
Palki (canopy)	Canopy. The structure that houses the Shri Guru Granth Sahib.
Pangat (pan-gat)	Row/line or group. Refers to everyone sitting together as equals without discrimination at the community kitchen found at all Sikh temples.
Panj Dosh (pun-j doo-sh)	The five thieves that all Sikhs should stay away from. Also known as the Panj Vicaar (five weaknesses).
Panj Gunh (pun-j gun-h)	The five qualities that Sikhs must work on developing in their lifetime in order to become closer and connected to Vaheguru.
Panj Kakkar (p-unj kaak-kar)	Five articles of faith that a baptized Sikh must wear. These are also known as the 5Ks.

Panj Pyare (p-unj pee-yar-e)	Five beloved ones. Refers to the first five baptized Sikh
Panj Vicaar (p-unj vee-car)	The five weaknesses that all Sikhs should stay away from. Also known as the Panj Dosh (five thieves).
Paramatma (pu-ram-at-ma)	Main soul. Refers to the name used by the Sikhs for G
Patka (pat-ka)	A head covering worn by Sikh children.
Piri (pee-ree)	Spiritual. Refers to the right sword found on the Sikh symbol known as the Khanda
Pyar (pee-yar)	Love. Refers to one of the five qualities that Sikhs must try to develop in their lifetime.
Raag (r-aa-g)	Beauty or colour. Refers to the rhythmic form in which the Sikh holy book is read.
Rabh (rab-h)	Lord/God.
Rehat Maryada (ray-hut mur-yaada)	The Sikh Code of Conduct that was formalized in 1945 by the Shiromani Gurdwara Parbandhak Committee. This is the elected governing body for the world's gurdwaras.
Rumala (roo-maa-la)	Decorative cloth to cover the Sikh holy book.
Sach Khand (s-ach kh-and)	True home. Refers to the resting room for the Sikh hol book during the night.
Sahej Paath (saa-hej p-aath)	Easy/slow reading of the Sikh holy book.

Sahejdhari Sikh (sa-hej-dari seek)	Easy/slow follower. Refers to a person who has chosen the path of Sikhi but has not yet been baptized.
Sahib (saa-hib)	A term of respect. It usually means sir or madam.
Sangat (sun-gat)	Congregation.
Santokh (san-tokh)	Contentment. Refers to one of the five qualities that Sikhs must try to develop in their lifetime.
Sarovar (saa-ro-var)	Pool. Refers to the pool surrounding the Shri Harmandir Sahib.
Sat (saat)	Truth. Refers to one of the five qualities that Sikhs must learn to develop in their lifetime.
Sat Naam (sat n-aam)	True name. Refers to the name used by the Sikhs for God.
Sat Shri Akal (saat sh-ree a-kaal)	Sikh greeting. It means "God is truth."
Seva (say-va)	Act of selfless/community service.
Sevadar (seva-daar)	Volunteer.
Shabad (shaa-baad)	Religious verse or scripture.
Shri (sh-ri)	A title of respect.

Shri Guru Granth Sahib (sh-ri goo-roo gr-aanth saa-hib)	Respected holy teacher or guidebook. This is the name of the Sikh holy book.
Shri Harmandir Sahib (sh-ri hur-man-dir saa-hib)	The most important Sikh temple, located in Amritsar, Punjab, India. Also known as the Golden Temple or the Abode/Home of God.
Singh (sing)	Lion. Refers to the middle name or surname of male Sikhs.
Tabla (tub-laa)	A small drum.
Takht (tu-kht)	Throne or seat of authority. Refers to the raised platform at the Sikh Temple on which the Sikh holy book is placed.
Vaheguru (waa-hay-goo-roo)	Wonderful God or a timeless being that never dies. Refers to the name used by the Sikhs for God.
Vaheguru ji ka Khalsa (waa-hay-goo-roo jee ka khal-sa)	Sikh greeting. Sikhs belong to Wonderful God.
Vaheguru ji ki fateh (waa-hay-goo-roo jee ki fa-teh)	Victory belongs to Wonderful God.
Vaisakhi (vay-saakhi)	Harvest festival.
Vand Ke Shako (v-and kay shaa-ko)	Share with the needy, sick, and less fortunate, and treat everyone equally. This is one of the three main Sikh principles or values.

Acknowledgments

It was an absolute honor to write this book.

First and foremost, I would like to thank Vaheguru for giving me the courage and strength to pursue my dream to write this book.

I also would like to extend a special thank-you to:

My beautiful daughter, Aniya (gift from above), for the inspiration to write this book when she asked me questions about Sikhi.

My husband Jack and son Jaylan for their support, guidance, and patience, and for always believing in me.

My dear mother, Harbhajan Kaur, for teaching me all about Sikhi. I was fortunate to have been introduced to this amazing and powerful gift at an early age. My faith in Vaheguru helped guide me through many challenging and difficult times in my life. I want to share this gift with today's children, so they can understand, appreciate, and embrace Sikhi.

My hardworking and courageous father, the late Jagir Singh, who taught me the principle of working hard and always doing the right thing (even when no one is looking).

My sisters Ravinder, Inderjeet, and Karenjit, and brothers Baljeet and Jagjit, for accompanying me on this adventurous journey known as life.

The late Dr. Raghbir Singh Bains, for his encouragement and for reading my very first manuscript.

Vivek Chowdhary (journalist), Basics of Sikhi (Southall, UK), Baltej Singh Dhillon, and all of my family and friends for their support.

Sukhwinder Kaur Basra

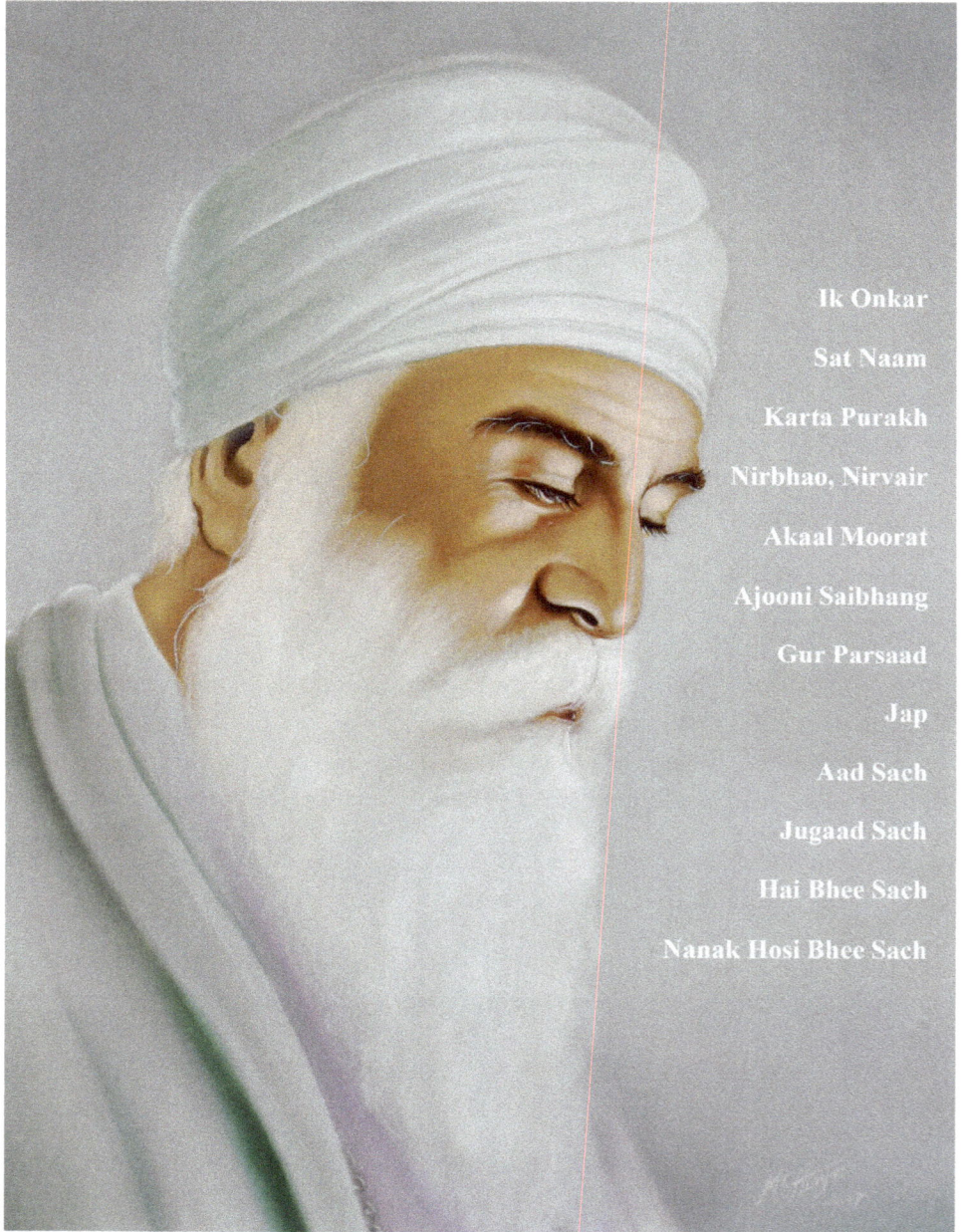

Ik Onkar

Sat Naam

Karta Purakh

Nirbhao, Nirvair

Akaal Moorat

Ajooni Saibhang

Gur Parsaad

Jap

Aad Sach

Jugaad Sach

Hai Bhee Sach

Nanak Hosi Bhee Sach

Lightning Source UK Ltd.
Milton Keynes UK
UKHW051251130121
376908UK00003B/52